PRINCES RISBOROUGH TO BANBURY

Vic Mitchell and Keith Smith

MP Middleton Press

Cover picture: The signalman of Princes Risborough North Box dutifully checks the train behind no. 7015 **Carn Brae Castle** *on 13th January 1962. Originating at Wolverhampton, it provided the only non-stop service from Princes Risborough to Paddington on weekdays, departing at 9.21am. (B.Jennings)*

**Published on the occasion of
the completion of the
redoubling of the route.**

Published September 2002

ISBN 1 901706 85 0

Design   Deborah Esher
Typesetting   Barbara Mitchell

Published by
          Middleton Press
          Easebourne Lane
          Midhurst, West Sussex
          GU29 9AZ
Tel: 01730 813169
Fax: 01730 812601

Printed & bound by Biddles Ltd,
          Guildford and Kings Lynn

INDEX

73	Ardley	48	Brill & Ludgershall
37	Ashendon Junction	42	Dorton Halt
82	Aynho Park Halt	21	Haddenham
90	Aynho Junction	32	Haddenham & Thame Parkway
99	Banbury	17	Ilmer Halt
58	Bicester North	93	Kings Sutton
53	Blackthorn	1	Princes Risborough

ACKNOWLEDGEMENTS

Our sincere gratitude goes to so many of the photographers who have helped us and also to A.E.Bennett, W.R.Burton, G.Croughton, F.Hornby, M.Dart, N.Langridge, Mr D. and Dr S.Salter, C.Stacey, D.Wilson, E.Youldon and, as always, our wives.

I. GWR map of 1910 (GWR Magazine)

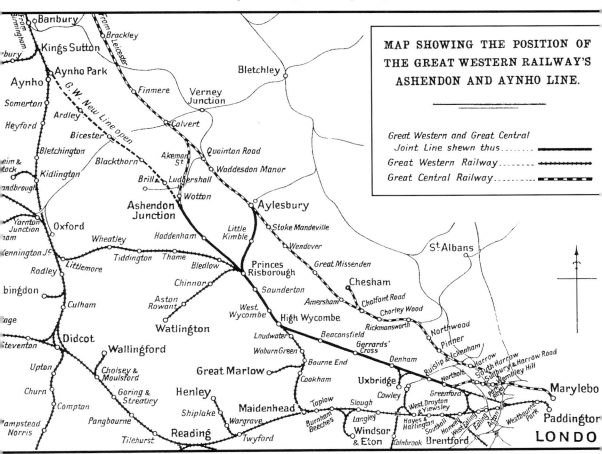

MAP SHOWING THE POSITION OF THE GREAT WESTERN RAILWAY'S ASHENDON AND AYNHO LINE.

Great Western and Great Central Joint Line shewn thus........
Great Western Railway..........
Great Central Railway..........

GEOGRAPHICAL SETTING

Princes Risborough is situated at the foot of the scarp slope of the Chiltern Hills and from here the line drops to cross the valley of the River Thame (not Thames), north of Haddenham. This section crosses Upper Greensand and Gault Clay.

Various outcrops of clays and limestones underlie the undulating route to Bicester. The River Ray, half a mile south of Blackthorn, is the only watercourse of note.

The remainder of the route is mainly associated with the Limestone of the northern extension of the Cotswolds. North of Aynho Junction, the line is in close proximity to the Oxford Canal and the south flowing River Cherwell.

The maps are at the scale of 25ins to 1 mile, unless indicated otherwise. North is at the top, except where there is an arrow.

II. Gradient profile.

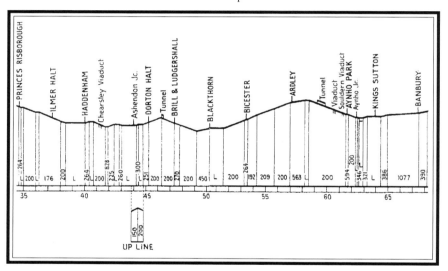

HISTORICAL BACKGROUND

The Wycombe Railway opened a single line broad gauge branch from the 1838 Maidenhead station to High Wycombe on 1st August 1854. It was extended to Thame on 1st August 1862 and a branch from Princes Risborough to Aylesbury was added in 1863. These lines were converted to standard gauge in 1870, having become part of the Great Western Railway in 1867. They were all operated by the GWR from the outset. A branch from Princes Risborough to Watlington came into use in 1872.

The Great Central Railway had gained access to its new terminus at Marylebone by

making arrangements in 1899 to run over the Metropolitan Railway via Aylesbury and Amersham. This was deemed to be unsatisfactory and so the GCR made plans with the GWR for a new joint line of double track south-east from High Wycombe to Northolt Junction. Here the GCR built eastwards, while the GWR laid double track to a junction with its 1838 main line.

The GWR had reached Oxford from Didcot in 1844 and the line was extended to Banbury in 1850 and on to Birmingham in 1852.

The GCR and GWR joint line north of Princes Risborough came into use on 20th

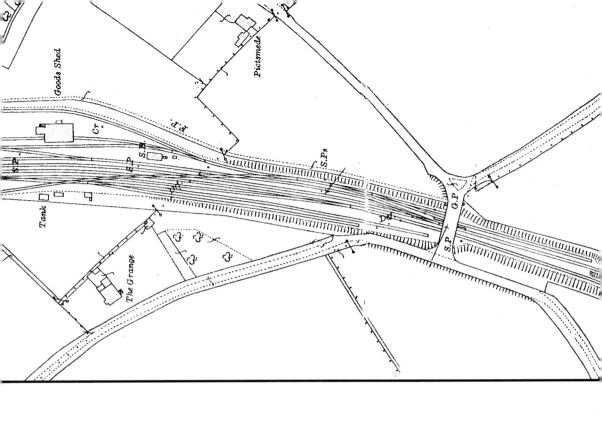

2.   There was a steady stream of freight trains between London and the Midlands. This example was recorded on 21st August 1948 behind no. 9018, a 3200 class renumbered from 3218 in 1946. Originally known as "Earls", the class was later nicknamed "Dukedogs". (J.H.Meredith)

3.   No. 5900 *Hinderton Hall* was a typical express locomotive, but the coaches were of Southern Railway origin. They formed the 10.10am Birmingham Snow Hill to Ramsgate service on 23rd July 1955. (H.C.Casserley)

4.   The station was extensively rebuilt in 1905 in readiness for its new main line status. Four through passenger lines were provided, plus one for goods (far left). Three bay platforms were available instead of one. The old station had three through platforms, plus one bay.
(The Lens of Sutton coll.)

5.   This view across the up platform includes the premises of Goodearls, makers of kitchen furniture. On the opposite side of the station there was a private siding from 1927 to 1971 for Forest Products Research Ltd. (Lens of Sutton)

6.　　The 4.34pm from Paddington (left) was hauled by a "Grange" class 4-6-0 on 23rd August 1961, while the connecting 5.44 to Oxford would leave behind 2-6-2T no. 6123. The signal in the centre is an ex-GWR lower quadrant, while the others are upper quadrant of GWR/GCR Joint origin. (H.Cowan)

7.　　Single railcars arrived in the area in April 1961. No. W55008 had worked the 7.45am from Banbury on 13th January 1962 and had been shunted onto the down through line to await the passing of the 6.45 Wolverhampton to Paddington, seen in the cover picture. The unit would then continue as the 9.37 stopping train to High Wycombe. (B.Jennings)

8.　　The east facade, photographed in October 1961, has changed little in almost 100 years. Beyond the two Ford saloons are the Aylesbury bay and North Box. The footbridge was demolished later. (B.Jennings)

9.   One of the few named autocoaches (*Wren*) stands at the up platform on 15th June 1962, having formed the 5.0pm from Banbury. On Fridays it did not arrive until 6.8, as it had to wait at Brill & Ludgershall Halt for 12 minutes for the 4.20 from Wolverhampton to pass and then for 18 minutes at Haddenham for "The Inter-City" to overtake. (B.Jennings)

10.   A Sunday morning train for Oxford waits on the left behind 2-6-2T no. 6124 on 20th May 1962, this service having only eight months left to run. Nos 42090 and 76038 were both from Neasden shed and were working engineering trains that day on the main line to Haddenham. (B.Jennings)

11.   The usual autocoach was not available on the last day of steam worked local train services from Banbury. The 11.5am departure was thus hauled by 5100 class no. 4112, which had to run round its coach upon arrival. Note the proliferation of telegraph wires. (B.Jennings)

12.   "Western" class diesel hydraulic locomotives were introduced to the route in June 1962; no. D1004 *Western Crusader* was recorded on 8th September of that year with the 6.30am from Birkenhead. At the platform is the 10.37 (Saturdays only) from Banbury. The last Birkenhead train ran in 1967. (B.Jennings)

13.   A train departs south on 6th August 1980 and passes the site of South Box, which had closed on 23rd September 1966. The down platform (right) had been taken out of use in September 1968 at the time of major track alterations and the fitting of a panel in the remaining signal box. The number of levers was reduced from 125 to 57 at that time. (B.W.Leslie)

14.   Further track changes took place in March 1991, since when all signalling has been undertaken at Marylebone. No. 58026 is working a ballast train on 11th July 1998 on the down through line. (M.J.Stretton)

15.   A new down platform was built over the site of the old down platform track and opened on 1st March 1999. No. 165014 was running from Marylebone to Birmingham Snow Hill on 11th March 2002. (M.Turvey)

Other photographs and maps of this station appear in our *Paddington to Princes Risborough* album.

16.   Seen in failing light on the same day is no. 168112, one of the new "Clubman" units with one class seating and air conditioning throughout. The new footbridge was provided with lifts for the less mobile. North Box was still standing in the background, having been given a listed structure status. The up track was signalled for reversible running. (M.Turvey)

ILMER HALT

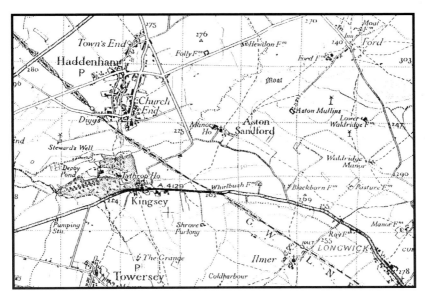

IV.   The tiny village and its halt are lower right on this 1945 edition of the
1ins to 1 mile map. The census return for 1901 showed 51 residents.

17.   The halt was constructed of timber and was opened on 1st April 1929. This view towards
Banbury was recorded some weeks before closure of the halt on 7th January 1963.
(The Lens of Sutton coll)

18. Glory days indeed! What could surpass the wonderful sight of a "King" at speed and working hard on the 1 in 176 climb up the foothills of the Chilterns? No. 6013 *King Henry VIII* was heading the 7.40am Birkenhead (Woodside) to Paddington on 2nd December 1961. (B.Jennings)

19. No. 6000 *King George V* was photographed near the site of the halt on 4th October 1971 with the "Return to Steam" special from Birmingham to Kensington. The Pullman coaches belonged to Bulmers and were kept at their cider factory in Hereford. (S.C.Nash)

20. New rails and new ballast were to be seen in the vicinity of Ilmer on 26th January 1998, as no. 165008 proceeded on its way from Marylebone (11.45) to Birmingham Snow Hill. (M.J.Stretton)

HADDENHAM

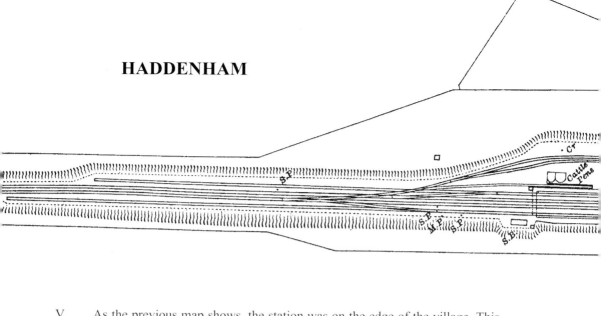

V.   As the previous map shows, the station was on the edge of the village. This had a population of only 1220 at the time of the planning of the line, and grew only slightly in the subsequent years. This is the 1922 edition.

21.   The 0-6-0ST is *Norman*, built by Hunslet in 1888. The mechanical diggers or "steam navvies" are on temporary broad track and have had their shovels removed. They stand with their beams vertical, having finished their work on the site. (Lens of Sutton)

23.   We now have another view towards Banbury, but this is from about 1930. It includes the post for the up main line home signal - only a board over a hole appears in the previous picture. There was a staff of ten here in the 1930s. (Brunel University/Mowat coll.)

24.   The 4.40pm from Paddington on 27th May 1939 departs after calling here at 5.45. No. 5080 was then still named *Ogmore Castle* and was later named *Defiant*. Sadly a negative fault obscures part of the station. The locomotive was eventually saved and subsequently resided at Tyseley Locomotive Works. (H.C.Casserley)

25.   Features of note included in this 1950s panorama are the perforated concrete signal post that had replaced the one seen in picture 23, the weighbridge office, the ramp of the end-loading dock and the parcels shed. (The Lens of Sutton coll.)

26.   We can now enjoy four photographs from 23rd April 1962. Beyond the parcels shed is the black framework of the cattle pens and the white painted loading gauges. Note that access to the goods yard was from the down main line. The yard closed on 2nd September 1963 and the 51-lever signal box followed on 18th April 1966, when the loops were taken out of use. (P.J.Garland/R.S.Carpenter)

———————▶

27.   A heated waiting room was provided on the down side, along with facilities for gentlemen only. However, the latter was devoid of a roof, but had two-tone glazed brickwork. (P.J.Garland/R.S.Carpenter)

Haddenham	1913	1923	1933
Passenger tickets issued	6810	5945	3251
Season tickets issued	7	82	51
Parcels forwarded	14473	13173	4855
General goods forwarded (tons)	1681	1003	185
Coal and coke received (tons)	113	17	36
Other minerals received (tons)	2225	2040	1035
General goods received (tons)	1344	1184	320
Trucks of livestock handled	31	61	18

———————▶

28.   Arriving at the up platform is 0-4-2T no. 1455 with autocoach *Wren*. The train is in close up in the next picture. The crane in the yard (right) was rated at five tons lifting capacity. (P.J.Garland/R.S.Carpenter)

29.   The timetable noted such trains as "Second class only" and showed up trains at 8.52, 12.4pm, 3.5, 5.57 and 6.53. These were Monday to Friday times and all terminated at Princes Risborough. There was also a 7.57am to Marylebone, but this was worked by a DMU. There was a Brackley to Marylebone service at 10.3pm. (P.J.Garland/R.S.Carpenter)

30.   It is 6th April 1962 and no. 6993 *Arthog Hall* is waiting with the 4.15pm Paddington to Wolverhampton, while the down "Birmingham Pullman" speeds past. Being a Friday, it was soon followed by the 5.10 from Paddington; the 4.20 Fridays only from Wolverhampton would often pass on the adjacent track at the same time; it is signalled in this view. (B.Jennings)

31.   Severe blizzards and a derailment had prematurely closed the line, but services were restored for the final day of Princes Risborough-Banbury stopping trains on Saturday 5th January 1963. The 3 Car DMU's extra accommodation was not required on the last services as with freezing weather the stations were hardly accessible. This is the 12.30pm from Princes Risborough in the worst winter in living memory. (B.Jennings)

HADDENHAM & THAME PARKWAY

32.   A single line passed through the countryside from November 1968 until 3rd October 1987 when a station was built almost half a mile west of the original. Its single platform is seen on 1st February 1998, as work began on creating a second one. (M.J.Stretton)

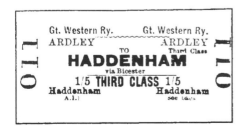

33.   One week later ducting was being laid as no. 165033 called while working the 11.45 Marylebone to Birmingham Snow Hill. The 1987 building is on the left and on the right is the 1930s airfield where glider pilots had been trained during World War II. (M.J.Stretton)

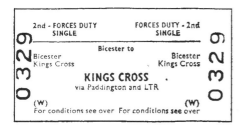

→

34.   On 15th May 1998, the new platform was being fenced in readiness for the second track coming into use on 24th of that month. A half-hourly service to London was provided in the basic timetable thereafter. (M.J.Stretton)

35.   No. 165027 had started its journey at Warwick Parkway (another new station) at 14.29 on 11th March 2002. The long approach path on the right is adjacent to the recently closed Haddenham Aerodrome. The unseasonal blooms in the hanging baskets are due to the skills of those in the plastics industry. (M.Turvey)

→

36.   An extensive car park and bus connections to Oxford, Aylesbury and Oakley were available when this photograph was taken in March 2002. Initially 160 car spaces were provided, but this had just been increased by 120. (M.Turvey)

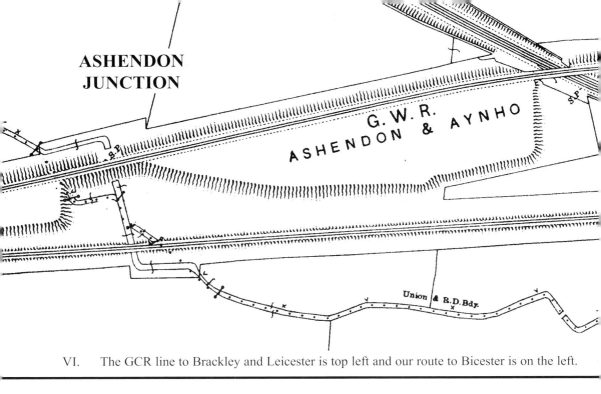

ASHENDON
JUNCTION

G.W.R.
ASHENDON & AYNHO

Union & R.D.Bdy.

VI.   The GCR line to Brackley and Leicester is top left and our route to Bicester is on the left.

37.   The 28-lever signal box was beyond the right border of the map, with its back to the GWR up single track. Seen in 1946, this box is opposite the zero milepost for the 1910 route to Aynho Junction. The flyover is in the background. (H.C.Casserley)

SOUTH OF BRILL & LUDGERSHALL

46.   No. 2368 was one of the 2300 "Dean Goods" class introduced in 1883. It is passing under the bridge that carried the Metropolitan Railway's Brill branch until December 1935. Part of the loading gauge of Wood Siding appears above it.. This and the next picture were taken on 22nd June 1935. (H.C.Casserley)

47.   No. 6017 *King Edward IV* was photographed from the bridge just described. It is about to enter the 191yd long Brill Tunnel with the 2.15pm Paddington to Wolverhampton. The branch bridge abutments were still in situ in 2002. (H.C.Casserley)

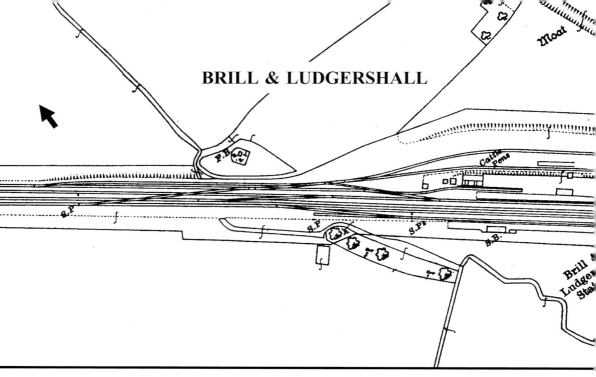

BRILL & LUDGERSHALL

VIII. The 1922 survey reveals a layout similar to that at Haddenham and Ardley. The previous map shows the relationship of the two villages to the station.

48. An early view towards Haddenham includes the parcels shed on the up platform. The population of Brill was recorded as 1206 in 1901 and 905 in 1961. Attempts to establish it as a spa town in the 19th century were unsuccessful; inadequate transport was a major problem. (Lens of Sutton)

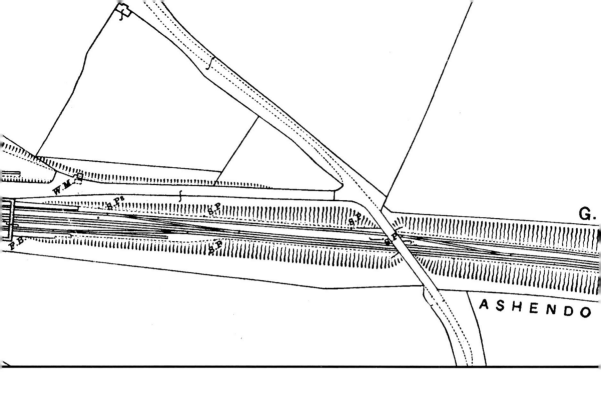

G.

ASHENDO

49.   The spacious signal box housed a 68-lever frame. It was in use from 28th June 1910 until 18th April 1966. The "S" and "T" boards were to indicate the need for the services of the travelling signal or telegraph engineer. It seems that the cycle engineer was already present.
(The Lens of Sutton coll.)

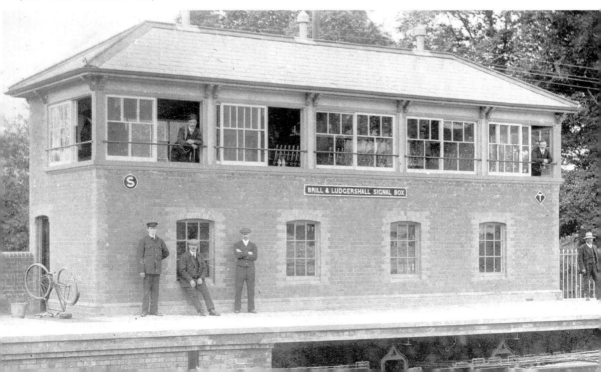

50.   On the right is part of the goods yard, which closed on 7th September 1964. Passenger trains ceased to call from 7th January 1963. (Lens of Sutton)

51.   We now have two panoramas from June 1962. This one is from the bridge carrying the road between the two villages and shows that the down refuge siding had been eliminated. The loops followed in April 1966. The up goods loop (right) had been shortened in April 1962. (P.J.Garland/R.S.Carpenter)

52.   Few passengers used the station, the service being similar to that listed at Dorton Halt. The station had been unstaffed since 2nd April 1956. (P.J.Garland/R.S.Carpenter)

BLACKTHORN

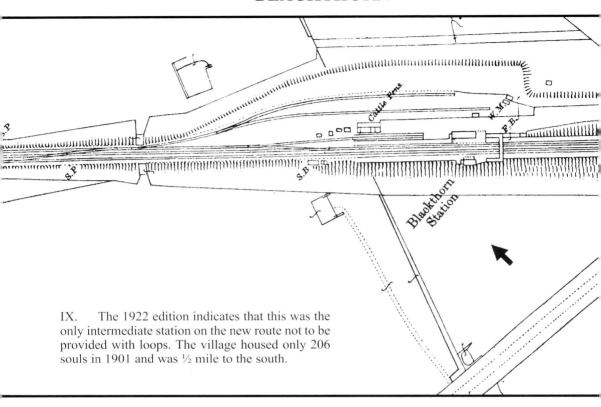

IX.   The 1922 edition indicates that this was the
only intermediate station on the new route not to be
provided with loops. The village housed only 206
souls in 1901 and was ½ mile to the south.

54. The station was closed to passengers on 8th June 1953 and to goods on 3rd January 1955. Only the shell of the up side building remained to be photographed on 16th June 1958. (R.M.Casserley)

←

53. This view towards Banbury includes a small corrugated iron parcels shed and the 21-lever signal box, which was in use from 27th June 1910 until 29th June 1958. However, it was often switched out. The platforms were shortened in 1931. (Lens of Sutton)

55.   No. 777 *Sir Lamiel* was working "The William Shakespeare" from Stratford-upon-Avon to Marylebone on 12th April 1986. Milepost 7 was ½ mile north of the site of the station. (S.C.Nash)

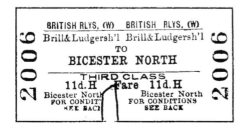

56.   This and the next photograph were also taken in Blackthorn Hill cutting, but on 15th May 1998 during track doubling work. The temporary siding accommodates no. 08646 with ballast wagons, plus a Fairmont tamper. (M.J.Stretton)

57.   Featured here is Trant Rail's Sollinger H and behind is a Newag ballast regulator. The line speed would soon be increased to 90mph and later to 100mph on both lines. (M.J.Stretton)

BICESTER NORTH

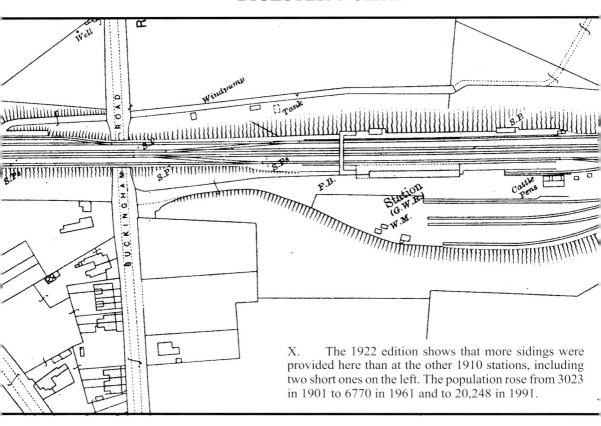

X.   The 1922 edition shows that more sidings were provided here than at the other 1910 stations, including two short ones on the left. The population rose from 3023 in 1901 to 6770 in 1961 and to 20,248 in 1991.

58.   The fully glazed footbridge had no intermediate support and was photographed shortly before completion. The market town already had one station, it being on the LNWR route between Oxford and Bletchley. It was known as "London Road" from 1954 until closure in 1968 and as "Town" when reopened in 1987. (Railway Gazette)

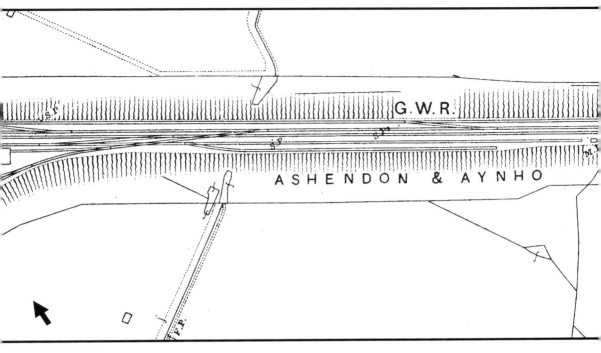

G.W.R.

ASHENDON & AYNHO

59.   A 1933 panorama includes a rake of cattle wagons near the goods shed. A water column was provided for locomotives standing on the up lines. The goods yard closed on 7th September 1964. The station suffix "North" was applied from 26th September 1949 until 1968 and again from 11th May 1987. (LGRP/NRM)

———————————→

60.   No. 5409 was working the 2.43pm Banbury to Princes Risborough on a grey day in July 1959. The milk tankers were fully braked for conveyance in passenger trains in this manner. They were glass lined. (H.Cowan)

61.   Slipping coaches at speed was practised widely by the GWR and the last in Great Britain was detached here from the 5.10pm from Paddington on 9th September 1960. The coach and its special double tail lamp was photographed on the previous day. The coach was taken forward by the 4.34pm semi-fast train from Paddington to Wolverhampton. The signal box had 67 levers and closed on 27th October 1968. (M.H.Walshaw)

———————————→

62.   The autocoach *Thrush* formed the Princes Risborough to Banbury stopping service on 28th March 1962, hauled by 2-6-2T no. 5101. Steam was in decline and an appropriate locomotive was not always available. Staffing of the station ceased on 2nd July 1962, but not for long. (D.Trevor Rowe)

63.   A loop with bidirectional lines was retained here after the 1968 singling. We stand beside no. 51894 which had left Marylebone at 10.35 on 1st April 1988 and watch no. 51665 working the 11.42 from Banbury. (T.Heavyside)

⟶

64.   Turning round, the photographer records a modest crowd and the facilities available at the sole remaining intermediate station. The stanchion-less canopy design was evolved around 1900 and this view shows that it involved placing the trusses right across the building. (T.Heavyside)

⟶

65.   A few minutes later and the Banbury train disappears into the distance and the London one is about to depart. Most services were provided by 4-car DMUs, one of the trailers of which was partially first class. (T.Heavyside)

66.   The route was regularly graced by steam locomotives of various origins from 1985 to 1990. Ex-LNER no. 4498 *Sir Nigel Gresley* hauled "The Peaks Express" from Marylebone to Matlock on 29th May 1989. (S.P.Derek)

→

67.   Ex-BR class 4 2-6-4T no. 80080 was recorded with its support coach on 14th July 1990 en route from its base at Butterley to the London Underground Depot at West Ruislip. From there it worked the "Steam on the Met" special trains. (S.P.Derek)

→

68.   "The Crompton Crescendo" avoids the loop on 1st February 1997. The demise of the class 33 "Cromptons" seemed imminent and thus the train was hauled by no. 33051 *Shakespeare Cliff* and no. 33116 *Hertfordshire Railtours*. The station received the Best Kept Small Station Award that year. (M.J.Stretton)

69.   A photograph from 3rd March 2002 features work in progress on the track doubling towards Banbury which was commissioned in August. A siding for terminating trains was laid where the van is standing and a new trailing crossover was provided soon after. The dog leg was a legacy from the previous layout. (M.J.Stretton)

70.   The exterior was well cared for when photographed on 10th June 2002. It had been adorned with Sugg's Windsor pattern lamps, although electrically lit. Picture 8 is the other one to include a complete Edwardian facade still extant on the route. (V.Mitchell)

71.   No. 165013 was working the 11.26 from Warwick Parkway on the same day and is seen passing some uncommissioned signals and one of three recent waiting shelters. The waiting room is from 1910. The new lift towers are included in this and the previous photograph. (V.Mitchell)

72.   The other two shelters were recorded a few minutes later as the 11.42 Marylebone to Birmingham Snow Hill arrived, formed of "Clubman" no. 168111. To the rear of it is a trailing siding for the engineers. (V.Mitchell)

ARDLEY

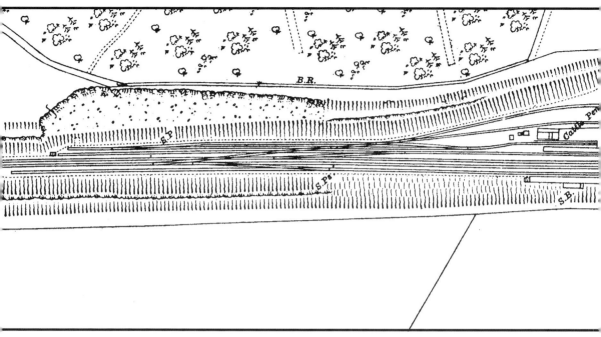

XI.   Here was another example of the excessive provision of facilities in a thinly populated district. There were 201 souls recorded in the village in 1901.

73.   Although the station was not complete, the signs for GENTLEMEN had been erected, presumably for the benefit of the contractor's workmen. The standard designs were employed here. (Lens of Sutton)

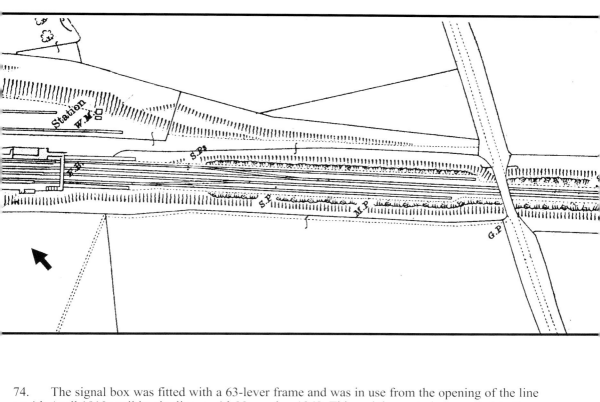

74.   The signal box was fitted with a 63-lever frame and was in use from the opening of the line on 4th April 1910 until its singling on 4th November 1968. This and the next photograph date from June 1962. (P.J.Garland/R.S.Carpenter)

75.   Staffing ceased on 1st August 1955 and alternative uses were found for redundant equipment. Sugg's Windsor design was still being manufactured in 2002, the press tool for the oak leaves dating from the 1870s. (P.J.Garland/R.S.Carpenter)

76.   Trains ceased to call after 7th January 1963, but freight facilities remained until 7th September 1964. Hopper wagons stand in the yard as limestone was loaded here from the adjacent quarry. (Lens of Sutton)

77.   No. D1694 and the up "Cambrian Coast Express" speed through the abandoned station on 11th May 1964. The procedure for recessing a long goods train (up to 80 wagons) was for it to run into the loop and into the siding beyond. The points at the rear would then be set for it to reverse into the one behind, such as that seen on the left. Other locations where this technique was employed can be seen in pictures 26 and 50. (M.Mensing/M.J.Stretton coll.)

78.　An abandoned platform is evident as a very special train passes through on 9th April 1988, during a snow shower. The area of control of Marylebone Panel was extended to this location in 1991. (D.Trevor Rowe)

79.　Westinghouse signal engineers acknowledge the driver's warning during preparatory work for the doubling on 28th February 2002. No. 168106 is working the 14.30 Birmingham Snow Hill to Marylebone service and is near the station site. (M.Turvey)

80.   The eastern portal of the 1147yd long Ardley Tunnel is in the background as no. 66547 works a ballast train on 3rd March 2002. It is adjacent to the trackbed that would soon receive new permanent way. The new rails are in the foreground and in the background is an aqueduct carrying a stream from a spring. (M.J.Stretton)

81.   No. 35028 *Clan Line* is on one of the two Souldern Viaducts with the 14.15 Stratford-upon-Avon to Marylebone on 9th June 1985. Their lengths are 400 and 580yds. (S.C.Nash)

AYNHO PARK HALT

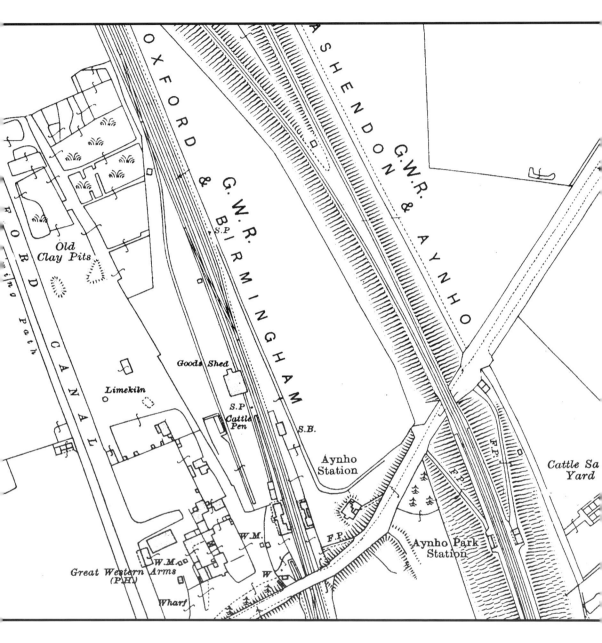

XII.   Our route is on the right of this 1922 map and the "station" is lower right. It was opened as "Aynho Platform", the GWR's term for a staffed halt.

82.   This 1932 view reveals that no suffix was shown on the nameboard. All structures were of timber to minimise weight on the embankment. Official opening was on 1st July 1910. (LGRP/NRM)

83.   Leaning on the curve, a "Castle" speeds through with an express for Wolverhampton in August 1960. The platforms were originally 400ft in length, but were shortened in 1961. (A.W.V.Mace/ Milepost 92½ Picture Library/R.S.Carpenter)

84.   The closure notice is on the door of the former booking office, which was at the end of the path to the up platform. This and the next picture are from June 1962. (P.J.Garland/R.S.Carpenter)

85.   The northward panorama from the foot of the path from the down platform includes the flyover carrying the 1910 down line over the 1850 route from Oxford. (D.Lawrence)

86.   This view is in the same direction, but from the ramp of the down platform as a down express approaches the flyover. Track singling commenced in this vicinity. (P.J.Garland/R.S.Carpenter)

87. A view from the down platform shortly before closure shows that provisions for gentlemen were retained to the end, despite lack of staff. The extent of the platform shortening is evident. (The Lens of Sutton coll.)

88. Unlike most of the closed stations on the route, this little used structure remained to be photographed in February 2002, together with its original railings. (M.Turvey)

89. A train from the South Coast to Sheffield was recorded from an autocoach from Princes Risborough as they both approached Aynho Junction in August 1960. The flyover is in the background. There had been loops on the 1910 lines in this vicinity until about 1917.
(A.W.V.Mace/Milepost 92½ Picture Library/R.S.Carpenter)

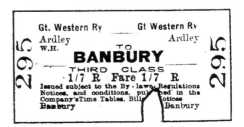

AYNHO JUNCTION

90.   Having descended the curve on the right, the autocoach will have passed behind the 39-lever Aynho Junction signal box. However, this indifferent southward view is from 1932. The box closed on 2nd April 1992, but was not demolished until July 2002. Its work was transferred to a panel in Banbury South box. (LGRP/NRM)

91.   The water troughs were 560yds in length and began 550yds north of the signal box. Using the down trough on 29th August 1962 is no. 6005 *King George II*. It is hauling the 5.10pm Paddington to Wolverhampton. (M.Mensing/M.J.Stretton coll.)

92.   Seen on the same day is the 4.40pm Wolverhampton Low Level to Didcot formed of three 3-car DMUs. The outer ones are of the suburban type while a cross-country unit is in the middle. The troughs lasted until 27th February 1967. (M.Mensing/M.J.Stretton coll.)

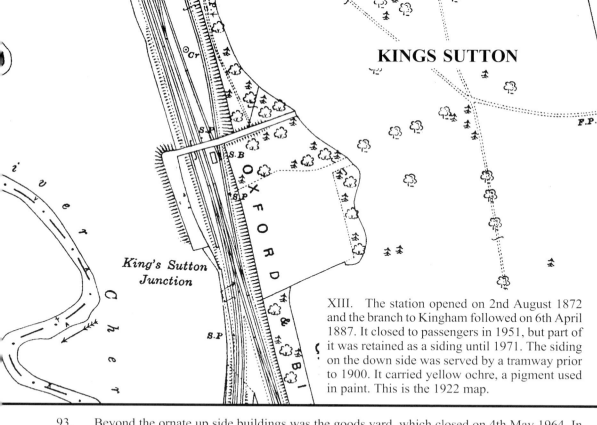

KINGS SUTTON

King's Sutton Junction

XIII. The station opened on 2nd August 1872 and the branch to Kingham followed on 6th April 1887. It closed to passengers in 1951, but part of it was retained as a siding until 1971. The siding on the down side was served by a tramway prior to 1900. It carried yellow ochre, a pigment used in paint. This is the 1922 map.

93.   Beyond the ornate up side buildings was the goods yard, which closed on 4th May 1964. In the distance is the 39-lever signal box, which was in use from 1887 until 4th April 1971. The population of the pleasant and peaceful village had risen to 1550 by 1961. (The Lens of Sutton coll.)

94. The 17.25 Banbury to Marylebone creeps away after stopping on 23rd July 1988, with the centre two coaches in NSE livery. Acceleration and exhaust emissions both improved with the next generation of DMUs. Staffing had ceased 20 years earlier. (P.G.Barnes)

95. No. 165009 calls on 28th February 2002, while working the 14.29 Warwick Parkway to Marylebone service. Such trains stopped here almost every hour at that time. There were also a few Thames Trains running via Oxford. NSE signs were still in place, eight years after its demise. (M.Turvey)

96.   No. 4919 *Donnington Hall* was recorded with a class C freight on 31st May 1963. This section of the route was close to the county boundary, the River Cherwell and the Oxford Canal. The M40 is also nearby nowadays. (B.W.L. Brooksbank/Initial Photographics)

97.   Two photographs from 26th October 1974 feature unusual motive power. The "Western" class was not employed frequently on freight work. No. D1044 *Western Duchess* is southbound with empties. The 29-lever Astrop Signal Box was in this vicinity and quadruple track ran from the north of it to Banbury. It closed on 16th September 1979. (T.Heavyside)

98.   No. 35028 *Clan Line* is working the Didcot to Stratford-upon-Avon leg of a railtour from Paddington on 26th October 1974. It continued via Cheltenham, Newport, Shrewsbury and Birmingham. The advertised return was "23.00, approx"! Note that the telegraph wires were still of the uninsulated type. (T.Heavyside)

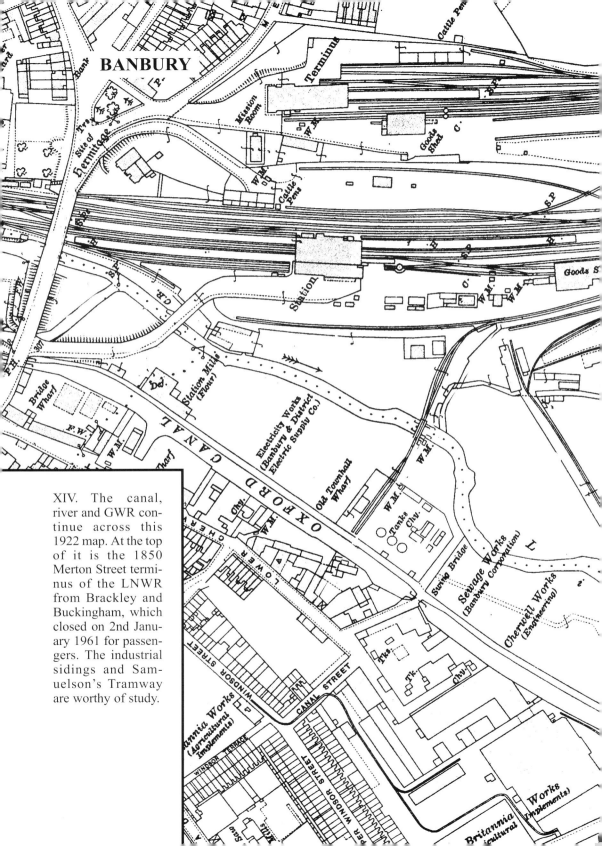

BANBURY

XIV. The canal, river and GWR continue across this 1922 map. At the top of it is the 1850 Merton Street terminus of the LNWR from Brackley and Buckingham, which closed on 2nd January 1961 for passengers. The industrial sidings and Samuelson's Tramway are worthy of study.

G. W. R.
OXFORD & BIRMINGHAM

...nia Works Depôt
(...gricultural Implements)

i v e r   *C h e r w e l l*

C.R.

F   *l*   *o*

b   *l*   *e*   *t*   *o*

Towing Path

HIGHTOWN ROAD

Allotment Gardens

CRESCENT

99.   This northward view through the train shed is from May 1933. The term "Banbury General" was in use from July 1950 to June 1961, but it was "Banbury Bridge Street" in Bradshaw for many years previously.
(Brunel University/Mowat coll.)

100.   No. 5947 *Saint Benet's Hall* was working the 2.38pm Leamington Spa to Oxford stopping train on 11th September 1937. The platforms had been lengthened and bays added in 1903.
(H.C.Casserley)

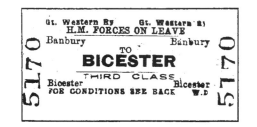

101.   The bay at the London end of the up platform was commonly used by the autotrain to Princes Risborough. The destination board is near the centre door. (The Lens of Sutton coll.)

102.   No. 4000 *North Star* was of the "Castle" class and on 15th March 1952 was relegated to the 1.20pm Birmingham Snow Hill to Paddington, which called at *all* stations to Oxford and many beyond, ending its amble at 5.55! (H.C.Casserley)

→

103.   Rebuilding had been planned in 1938, but it was delayed by World War II. The overall roof was removed in 1952 for safety reasons and replaced by these canopies as a temporary measure. (R.M.Casserley)

→

104.   The stopping service for our route was at the outer end of platform 4 when photographed with 0-6-0PT no. 5420 attached to autocoach *Thrush*. The shedplate is 84C, indicating that Banbury was its base. This bay was also used by trains to Kingham. (A.W.V.Mace/Milepost 92½ Picture Library/R.S.Carpenter)

108.   Class 08 no. D3107 is at work coupled to one of the shunters wagons peculiar to the GWR. They always carried the name of their allocated yard. Resting in the bay is no. 5947 *Saint Benet's Hall*. This platform was usually used by trains on the former GCR route from Woodford Halse until 5th September 1966.
(M.Mensing/M.J.Stretton coll.)

109.   An empty coal train leaves for the North, while no. 45004 runs south with vans on 27th July 1963. North of the station was an extensive marshalling yard, which was noted for forwarding large quantities of locally dug ironstone.
(D.Trevor Rowe)

110.   The photographers are active as the end of steam is nigh. No. 34005 *Barnstaple* is passing South Box on 3rd September 1966 with the 08.30 from Newcastle to Poole, where it was due at 18.55. It had run on the former GCR route via Leicester Central. (E.Wilmshurst)

115.   The station has been a convenient stopping point for steam specials on many occasions. No. 60800, an ex-LNER class V2, was on its way to participate in the Marylebone centenary celebrations when it stopped on the up goods line and was photographed on 6th March 1999. Bay platform no. 4 is on the left. (M.Turvey)

116.   No. 166204 was working the 12.39 Thames Trains departure for Paddington, calling at Oxford and Reading only. It is passing two of the few remaining semaphore signals on 11th June 2002. The engineers were using the sidings on the left; those on the right had served Dominion Oil. (V.Mitchell)

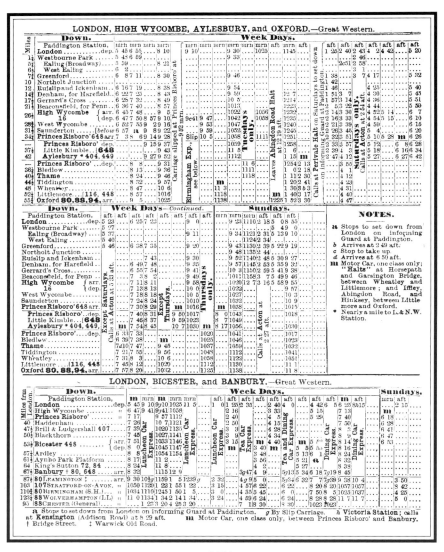

LONDON, HIGH WYCOMBE, AYLESBURY, and OXFORD.—Great Western.

LONDON, BICESTER, and BANBURY.—Great Western.

NOTES.

- **n** Stops to set down from London on informing Guard at Paddington.
- **b** Arrives at 2 49 aft.
- **c** Stop to take up.
- **d** Arrives at 6 59 aft.
- **m** Motor Car, one class only; "Halts" at Horsepath and Garsington Bridge, between Wheatley and Littlemore; and between Wheatley, Abingdon Road, and Hinksey, between Littlemore and Oxford.
- ***** Nearly a mile to L. & N. W. Station.

n Stops to set down from London on informing Guard at Paddington. **g** By Slip Carriage. **h** Victoria Station; calls at **Kensington** (Addison Road) at 8 29 aft. **m** Motor Car, one class only, between Princes Risboro' and Banbury.
† Bridge Street. ‡ Warwick Old Road.

1911

Gt. Western Ry.   Gt. Western Ry.
Brill & Ludgershall   Brill & Ludgershall
TO
BICESTER
6d **THIRD CLASS** 6d
Issued subject to the conditions & regulations set out in the Company's Time Tables, Bills & Notices
Bicester   Bicester

3958   3958

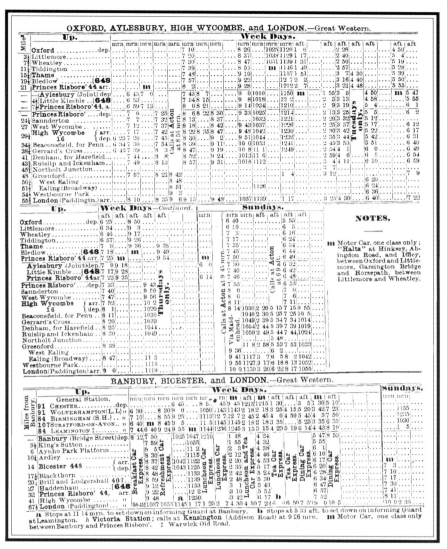

OXFORD, AYLESBURY, HIGH WYCOMBE, and LONDON.—Great Western.

Miles	Up.	Week Days. mrn	mrn	mrn	mrn	mrn (Calls at Acton at 8 55 mrn.)	mrn	mrn	mrn		mrn	mrn	mrn	mrn	aft		aft	aft	aft (Tuesdays only.)	aft		aft	aft
	Oxford ...dep.						7 10				8 26		1025	1120	1 6			2 28				4 50	
3¼	Littlemore						7 20				8 37		1038	1129	1 17			2 40				5 4	
7¾	Wheatley						7 30				8 47		1051	1139	1 31			2 50				5 19	
11¼	Tiddington						7 39				8 55		m	1146	1 40			2 57				5 28	
15¼	**Thame**						7 48				9 10			1157	1 51			3 7	4 30			5 39	
19½	Bledlow ...[648						7 57				9 22			12 7	2 2			3 16	4 40			5 50	
21	**Princes Risboro' 44** arr.			m			8 2				9 28			1212	2 7			3 21	4 48			5 55	
—	**Aylesbury** (Joint) dep		6 45	7 0			7 45	8 7			9 0	1010		1150	m		1 55	3 5		4 50		m	5 47
— 4½	Little Kimble ...[648		6 53				7 54	8 15			9 8	1018		12 2			2 3	3 13		4 58			5 55
— 7¼	**Princes Risboro' 44**, a.		6 59	7 13			8 0	8 21			9 14	1024		1210			2 9	3 19		5 4			6 1
—	**Princes Risboro'** ...dep.		7 0		7 25		8 6	8 22	8 30		9 33	1025		1214			2 13	3 25		5 5			6 2
24½	Saunderton		7 7		7 32		8 13		8 37		....	1032		1221			2 20	3 32		5 12			....
27	West Wycombe		7 12		7 37		8 18		8 42		9 43	1037		1226			2 25	3 37		5 17			6 12
29¼	**High Wycombe** 16 arr.		7 17		7 42		8 22	8 35	8 47		9 48	1042		1230			2 30	3 42		5 22			6 17
	dep.	6 25	7 20		7 45		8 30		9 2		9 51	1044		1232			2 35	3 44		5 42			6 31
34¼	Beaconsfield, for Penn	6 34	7 30		7 54		8 39		9 11		10 0	1053		1241			2 45	3 53		5 51			6 40
38¼	Gerrard's Cross	6 43	7 39		8 3		8 47		9 19		10 8	11 1		1249			2 54	4 1		6 0			6 49
41	Denham, for Harefield		7 44		8 8		8 52		9 24		1013	11 6					2 59	4 6		6 5			6 54
43¼	Ruislip and Ickenham		7 49		8 13		8 57		9 31		1018	1112					3 4	4 11		6 10			6 59
45¼	Northolt Junction																3 7						
48	Greenford		7 57		8 21	8 42								1 4			3 12						7 9
50¼	West Ealing					8 48														6 20			
51¼	Ealing (Broadway)					8 51						1126								6 24			
54¼	Westbourne Park					9 3														6 36			
55¾	**London** (Paddingtn.) arr.		8 10		8 35	9 6	9 15		9 48		1037	1139		1 17			3 25	4 30		6 40			7 22

Up.	Week Days—*Continued.* aft	aft	aft	aft	aft (Thursdays only.)			Sundays. mrn	mrn (Calls at Acton at 9 45 mrn.; Via Maidenhead.)	mrn	aft	aft (Calls at Acton at 6 9 aft.)	aft	aft	
Oxford ...dep.	6 25		8 50						6 40				5 55		
Littlemore	6 34		9 3						6 50				6 5		
Wheatley	6 46		9 17						7 3				6 16		
Tiddington	6 57		9 26						7 17				6 24		
Thame	7 9		9 36		9 38				7 35				6 34		
Bledlow ...[648	7 18		m		9 49				7 45				6 44		
Princes Risboro' 44 arr.	7 25	m			9 54			m	7 50				6 49		
Aylesbury (Joint) dep.	7 9	9 18						6 0	7 30				6 32		
Little Kimble ...[648	7 17	9 28							7 40				6 42		
Princes Risboro' 44 ar	7 23	9 35						6 14	7 46				6 48		
Princes Risboro' ...dep.	7 33			9 43					7 53				6 53		
Saunderton	7 40			9 50					8 0				7 0		
West Wycombe	7 47			9 56					8 6				7 6		
High Wycombe 16 arr.	7 52			10 2					8 11				7 11		
dep.	8 1			1020					8 14	1030	2 20	5 15	7 15	9 55	
Beaconsfield, for Penn	8 11			1030						1040	2 30	5 25	7 25	10 5	
Gerrard's Cross	8 20			1039						1049	2 39	5 34	7 34	1014	
Denham, for Harefield	8 25			1044						1054	2 44	5 39	7 39	1019	
Ruislip and Ickenham	8 30			1049						1059	2 49	5 44	7 44	1024	
Northolt Junction												5 48			
Greenford	8 38									11 8	2 58	5 53	7 53	1033	
West Ealing									9 36			6 2			
Ealing (Broadway)	8 47			11 3					9 41	1117	3 7	6 5	8 2	1042	
Westbourne Park				1115					9 55	1127	3 17	6 18	8 13	1052	
London (Paddington) arr.	9 0			1119					10 0	1130	3 20	6 22	8 17	1055	

NOTES.

m Motor Car, one class only; "Halts" at Hinksey, Abingdon Road, and Iffley, between Oxford and Littlemore, Garsington Bridge and Horsepath, between Littlemore and Wheatley.

BANBURY, BICESTER, and LONDON.—Great Western.

Miles from Banbury.	Up.	Week Days. mrn (Breakfast Car Express.)	mrn	mrn (Refreshment Car Express.)	mrn	mrn	mrn (Luncheon Car Express.)	mrn (Luncheon Car Express.)	m	aft (Luncheon and Tea Car Express.)	m	aft (Tea Car Express.)	aft (Tea Car Express.)	aft (Dining Car Express.)	m	aft (Dining Car Express.)				Sundays. mrn	mrn	
	General Station,																					
	91 Chester ...dep.				6 45		8 5	45	9 45	1215	1215	1 30	....	3 5	1 30	5 10						
	91 Wolverhampton (L. L) "	6 30		8 30	9 0		1050	1143	1143	2 18	2 18	3 25	4 15	5 20	3 42	7 23					1155	
	84 Birmingham (S.H.) "	7 10		8 55	9 25		1115	12 7	12 7	2 45	2 45	4 0	4 50	5 45	4 5	7 50					1235	
	107 Stratford-on-Avon "	6 40	m	8 45	9 5		11 5	1145	1145	2 18	2 18	3 35	....	5 25	3 35	6 35					1030	
	84 Leamington ‡ "	7 44	6 40	9 24	9 55	m	1144	1236	1245	3 15	3 15	4 29	5 19	6 14	4 43	8 19					1 5	
—	**Banbury** (Bridge Street) dep.	8 12	7 50		1025	1047	1210		1 48		4 24				5 47	8 53						
3½	King's Sutton		7 59		....	1055			1 55		4 32				5 55							
6	Aynho Park Platform		8 5		....	11 2			2 3		4 38				6 1							
10¼	Ardley		8 30		....	1115			2 12		4 46				6 10							
14	**Bicester 448** arr.		8 37		1042	1122			2 20		4 53				6 17					m		
	dep.		8 42		1043	1125			2 35		5 17				6 20					7 3		
17½	Blackthorn		8 48		....	1133			2 42		5 24				6 28					7 10		
20¼	Brill and Ludgershall 407		8 59		....	1139			2 48		5 30				6 34					7 17		
27	Haddenham ...[648		9 12		....	1153			3 1		5 43				6 47					7 30		
32	**Princes Risboro' 44**, arr.		9 22		....	12 2			3 10		5 52				6 57					7 41		
41	High Wycombe "		9 48		a	1230			3 42		6 17	b			7 52					8 11		
67½	**London** (Paddington) "	9h42	1037	1055	1145	1 17	1 25	2 7	4 30	4 50	7 22	6 [illegible]	6 50	7 59	9 0	10 5				10 0	2 35	

a Stops at 11 14 mrn. to set down on informing Guard at Banbury. **b** Stops at 5 33 aft. to set down on informing Guard at Leamington. *h* **Victoria Station**; calls at **Kensington** (Addison Road) at 9 26 mrn. **m** Motor Car, one class only between Banbury and Princes Risboro'. ‡ Warwick Old Road.

1911

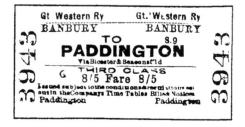

MP Middleton Press

Easebourne Lane, Midhurst, W Sussex. GU29 9AZ Tel: 01730 813169 Fax: 01730 812601
*If books are not available from your local transport stockist, order direct with cheque,
Visa or Mastercard, post free UK.*

BRANCH LINES
Branch Line to Allhallows
Branch Line to Alton
Branch Lines around Ascot
Branch Line to Ashburton
Branch Lines around Bodmin
Branch Line to Bude
Branch Lines around Canterbury
Branch Lines around Chard & Yeovil
Branch Line to Cheddar
Branch Lines around Cromer
Branch Lines to East Grinstead
Branch Lines of East London
Branch Lines to Effingham Junction
Branch Lines around Exmouth
Branch Lines to Falmouth, Helston & St. Ives
Branch Line to Fairford
Branch Lines around Gosport
Branch Line to Hayling
Branch Lines to Henley, Windsor & Marlow
Branch Line to Hawkhurst
Branch Lines around Huntingdon
Branch Line to Ilfracombe
Branch Line to Kingswear
Branch Line to Lambourn
Branch Lines to Launceston & Princetown
Branch Line to Looe
Branch Line to Lyme Regis
Branch Lines around Midhurst
Branch Line to Minehead
Branch Line to Moretonhampstead
Branch Lines to Newport
Branch Lines to Newquay
Branch Lines around North Woolwich
Branch Line to Padstow
Branch Lines around Plymouth
Branch Lines to Seaton and Sidmouth
Branch Lines around Sheerness
Branch Line to Shrewsbury
Branch Line to Swanage *updated*
Branch Line to Tenterden
Branch Lines around Tiverton
Branch Lines to Torrington
Branch Line to Upwell
Branch Lines of West London
Branch Lines around Weymouth
Branch Lines around Wimborne
Branch Lines around Wisbech

NARROW GAUGE
Branch Line to Lynton
Branch Lines around Portmadoc 1923-46
Branch Lines around Porthmadog 1954-94
Branch Line to Southwold
Douglas to Port Erin
Douglas to Peel
Kent Narrow Gauge
Northern France Narrow Gauge
Romneyrail
Southern France Narrow Gauge
Sussex Narrow Gauge
Two-Foot Gauge Survivors
Vivarais Narrow Gauge

SOUTH COAST RAILWAYS
Ashford to Dover
Bournemouth to Weymouth
Brighton to Worthing
Eastbourne to Hastings
Hastings to Ashford
Portsmouth to Southampton
Ryde to Ventnor
Southampton to Bournemouth

SOUTHERN MAIN LINES
Basingstoke to Salisbury
Bromley South to Rochester
Crawley to Littlehampton
Dartford to Sittingbourne
East Croydon to Three Bridges
Epsom to Horsham
Exeter to Barnstaple
Exeter to Tavistock
Faversham to Dover
London Bridge to East Croydon
Orpington to Tonbridge
Tonbridge to Hastings
Salisbury to Yeovil
Sittingbourne to Ramsgate
Swanley to Ashford
Tavistock to Plymouth
Three Bridges to Brighton
Victoria to Bromley South
Victoria to East Croydon
Waterloo to Windsor
Waterloo to Woking
Woking to Portsmouth
Woking to Southampton
Yeovil to Exeter

EASTERN MAIN LINES
Barking to Southend
Ely to Kings Lynn
Ely to Norwich
Fenchurch Street to Barking
Ipswich to Saxmundham
Liverpool Street to Ilford
Saxmundham to Yarmouth
Tilbury Loop

WESTERN MAIN LINES
Didcot to Swindon
Ealing to Slough
Exeter to Newton Abbot
Newton Abbot to Plymouth
Newbury to Westbury
Paddington to Ealing
Paddington to Princes Risborough
Plymouth to St. Austell
Princes Risborough to Banbury
Reading to Didcot
Slough to Newbury
St. Austell to Penzance
Taunton to Exeter
Westbury to Taunton

MIDLAND MAIN LINES
St. Pancras to St. Albans

COUNTRY RAILWAY ROUTES
Abergavenny to Merthyr
Andover to Southampton
Bath to Evercreech Junction
Bournemouth to Evercreech Junction
Burnham to Evercreech Junction
Cheltenham to Andover
Croydon to East Grinstead
Didcot to Winchester
East Kent Light Railway
Fareham to Salisbury
Guildford to Redhill
Reading to Basingstoke
Reading to Guildford
Redhill to Ashford
Salisbury to Westbury
Stratford upon Avon to Cheltenham
Strood to Paddock Wood
Taunton to Barnstaple
Wenford Bridge to Fowey
Westbury to Bath
Woking to Alton
Yeovil to Dorchester

GREAT RAILWAY ERAS
Ashford from Steam to Eurostar
Clapham Junction 50 years of change
Festiniog in the Fifties
Festiniog in the Sixties
Festiniog 50 years of enterprise
Isle of Wight Lines 50 years of change
Railways to Victory 1944-46
Return to Blaenau 1970-82
SECR Centenary album
Talyllyn 50 years of change
Yeovil 50 years of change

LONDON SUBURBAN RAILWAYS
Caterham and Tattenham Corner
Charing Cross to Dartford
Clapham Jn. to Beckenham Jn.
Crystal Palace (HL) & Catford Loop
East London Line
Finsbury Park to Alexandra Palace
Holbourn Viaduct to Lewisham
Kingston and Hounslow Loops
Lewisham to Dartford
Lines around Wimbledon
London Bridge to Addiscombe
Mitcham Junction Lines
North London Line
South London Line
West Croydon to Epsom
West London Line
Willesden Junction to Richmond
Wimbledon to Beckenham
Wimbledon to Epsom

STEAMING THROUGH
Steaming through Cornwall
Steaming through the Isle of Wight
Steaming through Kent
Steaming through West Hants
Steaming through West Sussex

TRAMWAY CLASSICS
Aldgate & Stepney Tramways
Barnet & Finchley Tramways
Bath Tramways
Brighton's Tramways
Bristol's Tramways
Burton & Ashby Tramways
Camberwell & W.Norwood Tramways
Clapham & Streatham Tramways
Croydon's Tramways
Dover's Tramways
East Ham & West Ham Tramways
Edgware and Willesden Tramways
Eltham & Woolwich Tramways
Embankment & Waterloo Tramways
Enfield & Wood Green Tramways
Exeter & Taunton Tramways
Greenwich & Dartford Tramways
Hammersmith & Hounslow Tramways
Hampstead & Highgate Tramways
Hastings Tramways
Holborn & Finsbury Tramways
Ilford & Barking Tramways
Kingston & Wimbledon Tramways
Lewisham & Catford Tramways
Liverpool Tramways 1. Eastern Routes
Liverpool Tramways 2. Southern Routes
Liverpool Tramways 3. Northern Routes
Maidstone & Chatham Tramways
Margate to Ramsgate
North Kent Tramways
Norwich Tramways
Reading Tramways
Seaton & Eastbourne Tramways
Shepherds Bush & Uxbridge Tramways
Southend-on-sea Tramways
Southwark & Deptford Tramways
Stamford Hill Tramways
Twickenham & Kingston Tramways
Victoria & Lambeth Tramways
Waltham Cross & Edmonton Tramways
Walthamstow & Leyton Tramways
Wandsworth & Battersea Tramways

TROLLEYBUS CLASSICS
Croydon Trolleybuses
Derby Trolleybuses
Hastings Trolleybuses
Maidstone Trolleybuses
Portsmouth Trolleybuses
Woolwich & Dartford Trolleybuses

WATERWAY ALBUMS
Kent and East Sussex Waterways
London to Portsmouth Waterway
West Sussex Waterways

MILITARY BOOKS
Battle over Portsmouth
Battle over Sussex 1940
Bombers over Sussex 1943-45
Bognor at War
Military Defence of West Sussex
Military Signals from the South Coast
Secret Sussex Resistance
Surrey Home Guard

OTHER RAILWAY BOOKS
Index to all Middleton Press stations
Industrial Railways of the South-East
South Eastern & Chatham Railways
London Chatham & Dover Railway
War on the Line (SR 1939-45)

BIOGRAPHY
Garraway Father & Son